IMAGES
of America

HERITAGE VALLEY

This early photograph of the Limoneira crew shows the new Mission Revival building Limoneira had erected in 1920 to replace the previous wooden structure. By the late 1920s, there were over 400 employees, and Limoneira had become the largest shipper of lemons in California. Santa Paula had become known as the "citrus capital of the world." (Courtesy of the Santa Paula Historical Society.)

ON THE COVER: Members of the Fillmore Fire Department are pictured with Chief Hume of the Fillmore Police Department in 1922. Hume was the longest-serving police chief in the United States until his retirement. (Courtesy of the John Nichols Gallery.)

IMAGES
of America

HERITAGE VALLEY

Evie Ybarra

ARCADIA
PUBLISHING

ISBN 978-1-4671-0553-8

Published by Arcadia Publishing
Charleston, South Carolina

Printed in the United States of America

Library of Congress Control Number: 2020934619

For all general information, please contact Arcadia Publishing:
Telephone 843-853-2070
Fax 843-853-0044
E-mail sales@arcadiapublishing.com
For customer service and orders:
Toll-Free 1-888-313-2665

Visit us on the Internet at www.arcadiapublishing.com

For Baby Eliot, taken from this world way too soon,
and for his sister Devon.

Also, for all of the descendants, relatives, and families of everyone who
settled in Santa Paula, Fillmore, Bardsdale, and Piru.
May you enjoy this look back into the past.

Contents

Foreword		6
Acknowledgments		7
Introduction		9
1.	Pioneers, Limoneira Ranch, and Union Oil	11
2.	St. Francis Dam Disaster	35
3.	Santa Paula Businesses and the Community	43
4.	Early History and Pioneers in Fillmore	77
5.	Rancho Sespe and Bardsdale	91
6.	Fillmore Community and Traditions	99
7.	Piru and Rancho Camulos	111
Bibliography		126
Index		127

FOREWORD

Return with me now to those thrilling days of yesteryear—yes, the yesteryears of our beautiful Heritage Valley, gracefully portrayed by local historian Evie Ybarra.

For those of us who were born here or have lived in the communities of Santa Paula, Bardsdale, Fillmore, or Piru for many years, the pages of this book are filled with images of familiar people and places. For those of you who are newer to the area, you'll likely say, "Oh, that's who that street/school/park/library was named after!"

The stories you will read sometimes are filled with wonder and mystery—like the tale of a child's remains rediscovered 65 years and hundreds of miles from where they were first laid to rest. What brought the pioneers to this valley? I am reminded of a phrase, "Before there was anything on the land, there was the land." All we have to do is gaze around us to understand the valley's allure.

I think my great-aunt Sarah Eliot Blanchard said it best:

> Father [Nathan Weston Blanchard] loved the wonder of this country; he would stand on the porch gazing across to Mupu Mountain—South Mountain—and exclaim, "This is a beautiful valley—a beautiful valley!" I looked at it thinking it was horrid, for all I saw was sagebrush, cactus, and oak trees, and I could distinguish nothing lovely about it. I have often wished since that I might see with fresh eyes, for now, I know how truly beautiful it is.

Betsy Blanchard Chess
Ventura, California
2020

Acknowledgments

Numerous members of the Santa Paula Historical Society have contributed hundreds of hours to preserve the history of Santa Paula and the Heritage Valley by organizing their photograph collection. Maggie Kimball has been very helpful and supportive of this project. Without her and the Santa Paula Historical Society, there would not be a book. The Santa Paula Historical Society maintains collections of archived research, photographs, and newspaper archives of the *Santa Paula Chronicle*, known today as the *Santa Paula Times*. All photographs in this book without a courtesy line are courtesy of the Santa Paula Historical Society.

John Nichols of the John Nichols Gallery spent many hours as photo editor of this book as he scanned photographs and shared his image archives. I also want to thank Craig Held, research librarian for the Santa Paula Blanchard Community Library, as he assisted in locating the right books and shared the archived files of the library. His wealth of knowledge was greatly appreciated, for it makes for interesting storytelling as well. Numerous families opened their photo albums and shared their private collections in order to present an accurate historical record of Santa Paula. Betsy Blanchard Chess shared numerous photographs and treasured family stories and heirlooms to help illustrate those stories.

The Smithsonian Institution and the Museum of American History allowed the photographs of my great-grandmother's exhibit to be shared in this book project. Thank you to Paula Johnson, Kay Peterson, and Steve Velasquez for all of their assistance in making it possible to share images from The Mexican Food Revolution exhibit, where my great-grandmother Concepción Sanchez's tortilla press, apron, and photographs are displayed. Dr. Susan Falck, executive director of the Rancho Camulos Museum, assisted with much of the research and photography. Rancho Camulos is so well-preserved, and it still resembles the way it looked in the late 1800s when the Del Valle family resided there. Great appreciation goes to Bob and Diana Cox for sharing their collection of Fillmore photographs as well as to Minnie Ybarra, Barbara and Ernie Leija, and Robert Ybarra for sharing their photographs of Fillmore and Olivelands. Thank you to Floreine Date for sharing her stories and Linda Starnes Faris for her photographs. Kristine and Mike Hyatt opened family albums and shared many of their archived family photographs. Elizabeth Michel shared her family collection of photographs, as did Tom Hardison. The Michels settled in Bardsdale, and Tom's family opened the Sanitary Dairy in Fillmore, which was a landmark business for many years. Rosie Romero Supina and Dr. Ofelia Romero Motlaugh shared stories and photographs, and for that, I am most grateful. I am most appreciative of the editors at Arcadia Publishing for assisting with this project. Thank you very much.

Of the many people who paved the way for this book through their research, Judith Triem and Mitch Stone willingly shared important stories of the Heritage Valley. The docents of the Museum of Ventura County and the research library were always gracious and had a smile whenever I asked for a research file—and they willingly made copies whenever appropriate.

Also, I want to thank my husband, Robert, for all of his encouragement and assistance through every aspect of this project. Our son Robert Jr. was supportive and assisted whenever I ran into a computer glitch. Thank you to my daughter Elizabeth and my son-in-law Chris for all of their encouragement and helpful critiques. Family is everything.

Thank you to the following contributors:

Elizabeth "Betsy" Blanchard Chess
Eva Leon Diaz
Linda Starnes Faris
Fillmore Historical Society
Robert Grosfield Sr.
Tom Hardison
Craig Held, research librarian, Santa Paula Community Library
Kristine Jaynes Hyatt
Barbara Ybarra Leija
Suzanne Lummis
Michelle McKinley
Dr. Ofelia Romero Motlaugh
Museum of Ventura County
John Nichols, John Nichols Gallery
Vincent Perez, historian
Dr. Alan Pollack
William Shiells
Mitch Stone, historian
Rancho Camulos Museum
Santa Clarita Valley Historical Society
Santa Paula Historical Society
Smithsonian Institution, Museum of American History
Rosa Romero Supina
Judith Triem, historian
Sharon Horn Villasenor
Lupe Ybarra
Robert John King Ybarra

INTRODUCTION

The journey through the rancho era takes one through the rich lands of the Santa Clara River Valley, known as Heritage Valley, including the "citrus capital of the world," Santa Paula and Limoneira Ranch. Nathan Weston Blanchard, known as the father of Santa Paula, and his business partner, Wallace Libbey Hardison, had the foresight to establish Limoneira. They used the Southern Pacific Railway to ship their citrus to the East Coast, competing with the Italian oranges sent by way of Florida. Wallace Hardison and Lyman Stewart founded the Union Oil Company, and the original building still stands on a corner of Main Street, where today it houses the Union Oil Museum.

When the early pioneers arrived in Santa Paula, it soon became apparent that they were competing for the use of the water. Julio Peralta was already in Santa Paula, and his homestead was near the Santa Paula Creek, which provided all the water he needed for his ranch and trees. Soon, there was a legal battle over water rights. Peralta, a member of the Mexican elite, had been granted his land by the Mexican government. After having paid four attorneys, one being Reynaldo "Reginald" Del Valle of Rancho Camulos, he won his lawsuit and was awarded water rights to the Santa Paula Creek. But the new ranchers ignored the court ruling, and diverted water away from Peralta's land. The ruling was not enforced. Peralta ran out of money, and decided to leave the area.

Rancho Sespe, on the outskirts of Fillmore, was originally purchased by T. Wallace More, who was murdered over water rights and land claims. More purchased the land, and resented the squatters taking over land they had not legally acquired. After More's death, his wife, Susannah, became owner of the land. She passed away two years later. Morton Hull of Chicago purchased Rancho Sespe and gave the land to his twin children, Morton and Eudora. (They had the same names as their parents.) After Eudora married Keith Spalding of the sporting goods company, they purchased Morton's share of the land and owned all of Rancho Sespe. Nearby, the communities of Fillmore and Bardsdale were developed, and many citrus orchards were planted in the area. In Fillmore, the Sanitary Dairy was established by the Hardison family and prospered through 1977, when Russell Hardison retired. Sanitary Dairy trucks delivered milk to the schools and to the community of Rancho Sespe for many years. Movie companies have filmed in the Fillmore, Bardsdale, and Rancho Sespe areas. *The Philadelphia Experiment* and *La Bamba* were filmed along Central Avenue and in rural Bardsdale.

Piru and Rancho Camulos are just down Highway 126, approximately eight miles from Fillmore. The legendary Piru Mansion can be seen nestled against the hills in Piru from Highway 126. Today, the Rancho Camulos Museum is well-preserved as a historical landmark and resembles its original condition from the 1880s. Helen Hunt Jackson visited Rancho Camulos in the 1880s and based her novel *Ramona* on the location.

Jacob Michel was one of the first to purchase Bardsdale acreage, and family members continue cultivating their citrus fruit there today. The Sespe backcountry is very much a part of the Heritage Valley, and the California condor can be found there. The Chumash Indians populated the Sespe, Fillmore, and Santa Paula regions. The very fortunate may still find Chumash relics.

One

Pioneers, Limoneira Ranch, and Union Oil

The luscious Santa Paula area and its surrounding valley is one of the most beautiful vistas to behold. Looking south toward South Mountain, one can make out the image of the Lady of South Mountain, a famous Native American legend of the area. Santa Paula boasts the world-famous Limoneira Ranch, the Glen Tavern Inn, the Union Oil Museum, the Agriculture Museum, and the Santa Paula Gallery of Art. Many films have been made here, as well as well-known commercials. The Blanchard Community Library is a product of the generous donation of Nathan Weston Blanchard and his wife, Ann Hobbs Blanchard. It was originally named the Dean Hobbs Blanchard Memorial Library as a tribute to their young son who passed away at five years of age.

In 1851, the US government informed all landowners that proof of ownership was now required, as was having their land surveyed and marked. Titles would have to be presented and approved. It was a difficult time for the Mexican landowners because many did not have the proof, nor did they have all their land surveyed. To complicate matters, the courts were ineffective and too slow to remedy all of the contested issues of ownership. Mexican landowners began losing their acreage or lost their money fighting in the courts. Homesteaders and squatters came, following the new guidelines and claiming the land as their own, cultivating and building on it.

The newcomers diverted the water they needed to irrigate their crops. T. Wallace More proclaimed that the land was his and that he had paid for it at the Santa Barbara auction and that the others were trespassers. The US land commission decided in his favor, but later, its decision was overturned. This allowed the squatters to homestead open lands in Rancho Sespe. Settlers came into the Santa Paula and Fillmore-Bardsdale areas, and new communities were born.

Nathan Weston Blanchard planted the first citrus crop in Santa Paula. Early in 1854, he arrived in California and soon moved to Ventura County, which was then part of Santa Barbara County. He was elected to the state legislature from Placer County and served from 1862 to 1863. In 1872, he purchased part of a land grant from E.B. Higgins, and together they engaged in ranching and sheep raising. They set up a flour mill, which used water from Santa Paula Creek. Blanchard named the new town Santa Paula, laying it out in 1873. He planted the first citrus orchards in 1874, and pioneered the citrus industry in the Santa Clara Valley—Heritage Valley.

Nathan Weston Blanchard married Ann Elizabeth Hobbs on December 21, 1864. She was a native of New Berwick, Maine. They had five children: Dean Hobbs, Sarah Eliot, Eunice Weston, Nathan Weston Blanchard Jr., and Thomas Hobbs. Their first and last children died very young. The couple engaged in general ranching and sheep raising. A flour mill was built by Nathan Blanchard and his silent partner from Placer County, Elisha L. Bradley. Blanchard and Bradley bought out E.B. Higgins, and they raised sheep and alfalfa as well as experimenting with other crops.

Main Street in Santa Paula is seen here in the early 1900s when Santa Paula became a community. (Courtesy of the Craig Held family.)

The Main Street depot was the center of town as soon as the Southern Pacific Railway came through, and transportation by railway became popular.

Seen here is the flour mill that Nathan Weston Blanchard established with Elisha L. Bradley after they bought out E.B. Higgins. They were able to obtain and utilize water rights from the nearby Santa Paula Creek.

The Goldstein Building is seen in this view of Santa Paula's Main Street.

Wallace Libbey Hardison founded the Union Oil Company with his partner Lyman Stewart and was also engaged in the citrus industry in Santa Paula. He owned the *Los Angeles Herald* for four years. He had a son, Guy, and two daughters, Augusta and Hope. He left his wife of 20 years and remarried, living in Pasadena. On April 10, 1909, a locomotive crashed into Hardison's automobile at the Monte Vista railroad crossing, killing him.

The Hardison family left their imprint on the citrus and petroleum industries in Santa Paula and throughout the nation.

Charles H. McKevett was an important part of the town's beginnings, as he bought up real estate and helped develop housing. The town of Santa Paula grew, and McKevett donated land for a school, the McKevett School, which is still used today.

The Union Oil Building serves as the Union Oil Museum today. Wallace Hardison established his office on the second floor of this building when he set up Union Oil with Lyman Stewart and Thomas Bard.

Thomas Bard was one of Nathan Weston Blanchard's best friends, and the two families shared many joyous times together. His family lived at Berylwood in Port Hueneme.

Royce G. Surdam worked for Thomas Bard and served as the first postmaster in Bardsdale. He assisted Bard with the purchase of land in Santa Paula and Bardsdale.

This oil well belonging to Thomas Bard was the first successful well in the area. It was north of Sulphur Mountain.

A jackline was used to pull oil up from the deep well. It was driven by a 25-horsepower engine.

Trains made regular trips on the Southern Pacific from Ventura to Santa Paula, Fillmore, and Piru to Los Angeles. The citrus crops would be loaded on railcars for delivery to the Los Angeles market and other parts of the United States. Passengers also boarded the train here.

Wallace Hardison and Lyman Stewart purchased the Mission Transfer Company and Refinery. It owned the mineral leases on Sulphur Mountain. The refinery was later part of the Union Oil Company.

Torrey Canyon Field was purchased by Lyman Stewart and Wallace Hardison as part of the Union Oil Company.

Lyman Stewart designed a tanker to transport oil to the refinery in San Francisco in an attempt to convince the Southern Pacific Railway to lower its rates. The tanker was only in service for a few months before it caught fire at the Ventura wharf. Southern Pacific did lower its rates.

Herman Keene was an avid outdoorsman and hunter. Here, he is pictured with his most recent bounty of mountain lions.

This photograph, taken in 1924 in the hills above Santa Paula, shows the Ku Klux Klan during one of its rituals. Most everyone in Santa Paula was a member of the organization at that time, but later, the Klan fell out of favor because it was interfering with citrus profits. The KKK terrorized the Mexican men who were employed to pick the crops, and many would leave the fields early to avoid trouble. By the 1930s, the Klan had disappeared from Santa Paula.

This was the view looking south from McKevett Hill in 1888. The arrival of the Southern Pacific brought travelers and freight to the area.

The Limoneira headquarters was built as the company was expanding and exporting oranges and lemons. Santa Paula was known as the "citrus capital of the world."

As the citrus crops increased, Limoneira's lemon and orange exports grew. The company utilized advanced mechanization in its processing plant and provided uniforms for the workers.

The Limoneira store assisted all the farmworkers and their families because their homes were far from the center of town. The farmworkers lived in a rural area of Santa Paula, known today as the Olivelands area.

This citrus packing label was used by the Limoneira Company in the 1920s. Today, original labels like this are rare.

The lemon house of Limoneira was one of the most important buildings on the ranch property.

Women worked in the Limoneira packinghouse sorting and packing fruit during World War II, as the men had enlisted in the armed services. While they served their country, their mothers, sisters, and wives worked back home.

The Limoneira camp was divided up according to ethnic groups, and this is what the farmworkers preferred at the time. The people lived amicably and worked together without any racial issues or problems.

The Limoneira rowhouses shown here were where the families lived. A similar setup could be found in Rancho Sespe, about 10 miles east on Highway 126.

This crew is sorting and packing lemons. Originally, the workers at the Limoneira Ranch were all Chinese men.

This is an overview of the Billiwhack Ranch and Dairy. The land was originally purchased by August Rubel, who built a dairy on the property in 1924–1925. At about the same time, he also purchased Rancho Camulos, where he moved his family to live while he was in preparation for the dairy's production. (Courtesy of the Craig Held family.)

Seen here is production at the Billiwhack Dairy in the 1940s. The Fratkin brothers, Sam and Ben, owned the Valley Dairy company of Los Angeles, and that company purchased Billiwhack Dairy. (Courtesy of the Craig Held family.)

Billiwhack Dairy was purchased by the Held family. Here is a photograph of the entire crew on the property. The hedge has been trimmed to spell the name "Billiwhack." (Courtesy of the Craig Held family.)

Workers on the Jauregui Ranch brand one of the sheep. The Jauregui family purchased property in Wheeler Canyon, and their sheep would be seen roaming the hillsides from the edge of Ventura to Santa Paula.

The Briggs Packing House also became part of the Limoneira Ranch enterprise. By the 1920s, there were five additional packing plants in Santa Paula. Briggs was adjacent to the railroad.

The Olivelands School was built by the Limoneira Company for the purpose of educating the farmworkers' children. It was in close proximity to the homes of the workers' families. (Courtesy of the Minnie Ybarra family.)

Seen here at Ventura Beach are the teaching staffs of Olivelands and Briggs Schools, both on the west side of Santa Paula. Included are Beatrice Albright, Anne Lincoln, Lois Sparks, Persis Hamilton, Anne Morsoff, Nixon Wells, Mary L. Galvin, Maizie Lewis, Margaret Cross, Catherine Hurley, Evelyn Houston, and Betty Vig. (Courtesy of the Minnie Ybarra family.)

The Blanchard Library is seen in its original form in Santa Paula on the corner of Main and Eighth Streets. (Courtesy of the Betsy Blanchard Chess family.)

Sarah Blanchard is pictured here. She chronicled her life in several diaries and wrote a book about growing up in Ventura County. She served as the first president of the Dean Hobbs Blanchard Memorial Library board in 1911, and is the author of *Memories of a Child's Early California Days*, published in 1961.

El Naranjal is the name that was given to the Nathan Weston Blanchard family home in Santa Paula. Sarah Blanchard remained there after Nathan's death, and lived in the family home throughout her life.

Nathan Weston Blanchard Jr. married Esther Byrd, and they had three sons: Nathan Weston Blanchard III, Dean Hobbs Blanchard, and Eliot McClelland Blanchard. Esther was described as a lovely lady who earned the nickname "Grandma Tiny" from her grandchildren because she was so petite, at four feet, ten inches. Betsy Blanchard Chess reminisced that her grandmother had a sunny disposition, a beautiful voice, and was beloved by everyone. (Courtesy of the Betsy Blanchard Chess family.)

Eliot McClelland Blanchard, born in 1914, was the third son of Nathan and Josephine Blanchard. He attended the Thacher School and graduated from Stanford University in 1936. In 1937, he married Elizabeth Irene Munger. Eliot enrolled in Stanford Law School, while Elizabeth studied for her bachelor of arts degrees in journalism, economics, and history; they both graduated in 1939. After practicing law in Beverly Hills, Eliot enlisted in the US Navy in 1941, serving as a first lieutenant in the Pacific during World War II. Elizabeth returned to Santa Paula, and after the war, Eliot managed the Samuel Edward Associates' ranching and oil properties. Eliot was active in community organizations and was a member of numerous county boards. The couple had three children: James Eliot Blanchard, John William Blanchard, and Elizabeth "Betsy" Blanchard Chess. (Courtesy of the Betsy Blanchard Chess family.)

Elizabeth Munger Blanchard is pictured on her wedding day in 1937. While attending Santa Paula High School, she served as student body vice-president and editor of the yearbook and school newspaper. She attended Holmby College in Los Angeles for two years before returning to Santa Paula. She taught briefly at Balboa Junior High in Ventura and served on the Santa Paula Elementary School board, and on the Santa Paula High School board for many years. She served on the county Juvenile Justice Commission for 22 years and was president of the board of directors of the Museum of Ventura County. She was selected the Santa Paula Chamber of Commerce Citizen of the Year in 1983 and was honored as grand marshal of the Santa Paula Festival. (Courtesy of the Betsy Blanchard Chess family.)

Minnie and Marcelino "Woody" Ybarra celebrate their wedding at the Blanchard residence on December 31, 1949. From left to right are Elizabeth Blanchard, Minnie and Woody, and Eliot Blanchard holding his daughter Betsy. Elizabeth provided a home for Minnie while Eliot was away serving during World War II, and she cared for their two boys, Jim and John. (Courtesy of the Minnie Ybarra family.)

Elizabeth Blanchard poses with her three children (from left to right), Jim, Betsy, and John. (Courtesy of the Betsy Blanchard Chess family.)

Two

St. Francis Dam Disaster

The St. Francis Dam broke three minutes before midnight on March 12, 1928. Ace Hopewell was riding his motorcycle up the San Francisquito Canyon road on his way to powerhouse No. 1 of the Los Angeles Bureau of Power and Light. The dam had been completed two years earlier under the authority of Los Angeles Water chief William Mulholland, and five days earlier, it was filled to capacity. Mulholland had been hired by the Sespe Land and Water Company in 1888 to lay out the water pipes for the city of Fillmore. He had completed the aqueduct project, which brought water from the Owens Valley to the Los Angeles area, and then directed the construction of a series of dams in Los Angeles. Ace Hopewell, riding up the canyon, heard a crashing sound coming from the dam, which was behind him. He continued up the canyon to the powerhouse, where he learned that the dam had given way, spilling 12 billion gallons of water. A 180-foot-high wall of water rushed down the valley. The billions of gallons traveled down the San Francisquito Canyon, through the Santa Clarita Valley, and down the Santa Clara River Valley to the Pacific. It drowned an estimated 600 people and devastated portions of Piru, Bardsdale, Fillmore, Rancho Sespe, Santa Paula, and Saticoy. There were 66 unidentified victims, and 18 are buried in the Santa Paula Cemetery. Ann Stansell, a student at California State University, Northridge, compiled historical information about the St. Francis Dam Disaster, and was instrumental in establishing the St. Francis Dam Memorial in Santa Clarita, California. The Santa Paula Historical Society erected a memorial for the 18 unidentified victims. The remaining 48 graves are on the east end of Ivy Lawn Cemetery in Ventura.

This is the St. Francis Dam in San Francisquito Canyon during construction. William Mulholland was the engineer, and Harvey Van Norman was the second in command. Mulholland accepted the blame for the disaster but was never prosecuted. Van Norman returned to Santa Paula and helped direct the cleanup efforts and rebuilding of bridges along the Santa Clara River. He lived at the Glen Tavern Inn for three months after the disaster. (Courtesy of the John Nichols Gallery.)

The Isbell School was damaged in the flooding. It had been dedicated two years earlier, named after Isbell Mann, the first teacher in the state of California. She and her husband moved to Santa Paula after having lived in Santa Clara. (Courtesy of the John Nichols Gallery.)

The Isbell School is seen here surrounded by mud and debris. (Courtesy of the John Nichols Gallery.)

No community in the Heritage Valley escaped the disaster. Over 600 people perished. (Courtesy of the John Nichols Gallery.)

Joe Gottardi searches for his family after the St. Francis Dam disaster. Those who perished included his wife, Frances, along with sons Joe, Reno, and Richard and daughters Lenore and Pauline. (Courtesy of the Santa Clara Valley Historical Society.)

This search and rescue team had the grim task of recovering bodies and washing the mud from them so they could be identified. Undertakers from San Luis Obispo, Santa Barbara, and Los Angeles Counties arrived to help with the embalming. (Courtesy of the John Nichols Gallery.)

Searchers discovered the body of this young man among the debris and mud. (Courtesy of the John Nichols Gallery.)

Crews would take the bodies to be hosed down and cleaned prior to moving them to one of the makeshift morgues in town. The Santa Paula depot served as a morgue for many after the disaster. (Courtesy of the John Nichols Gallery.)

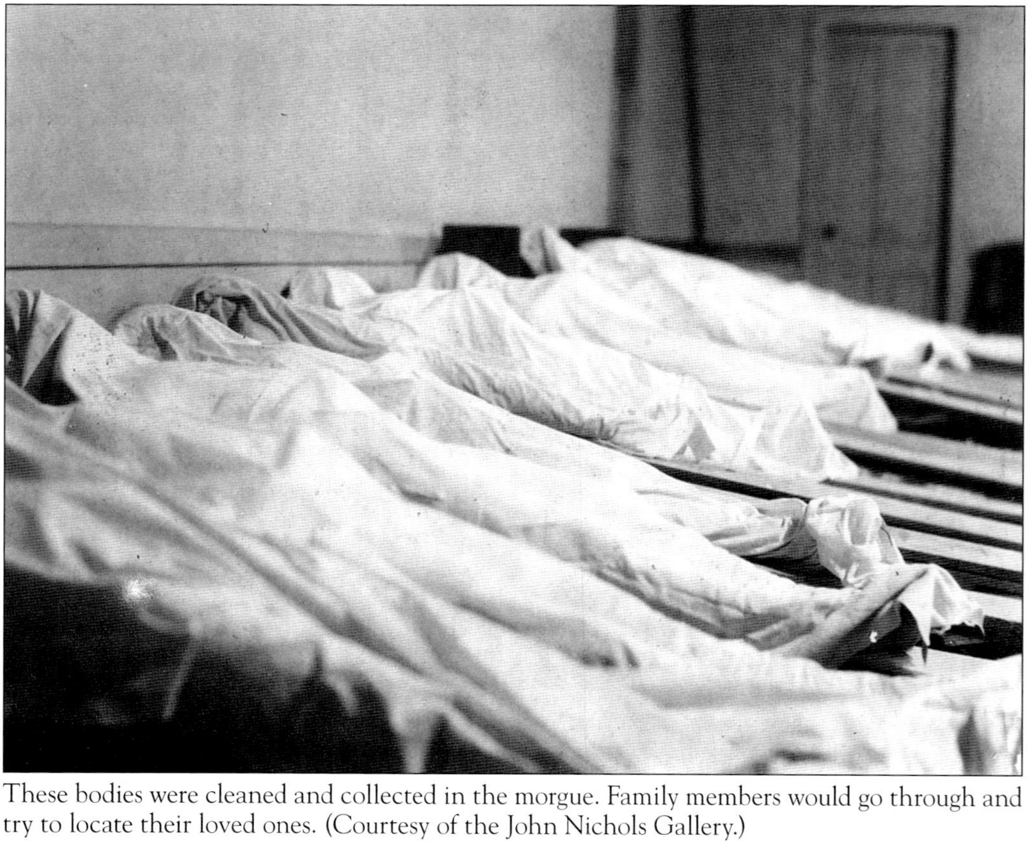

These bodies were cleaned and collected in the morgue. Family members would go through and try to locate their loved ones. (Courtesy of the John Nichols Gallery.)

'All the News 'All the Time'

LARGEST HOME-DELIVERED CIRCULATION LARGEST ADVERTISING VOLUME

Los Angeles Times

In Three Parts — 44 Pages

Equal Rights

Liberty Under the Law — True Industrial Freedom

Vol. XLVII. WEDNESDAY MORNING, MARCH 14, 1928. DAILY, FIVE CENTS SUNDAY, TEN CENTS

200 DEAD, 300 MISSING, $7,000,000 LOSS IN ST. FRANCIS DAM DISASTER

Plane Views Give Idea of Magnitude of Catastrophe

Left—View of the wrecked St. Francis Dam taken from the air at a point just below the dam. Right—Santa Paula, as seen from the air. Directly in the path of the raging torrents, portions of the city were inundated. [Photographs taken by Harry C. Anderson, Times staff photographer.]

THOUSANDS RUSH TO AID IN WORK OF RESCUE AND RELIEF

Red Cross Directs Gigantic Task of Succor in Devastated Area; Water Board Appropriates $25,000; Food and Shelter Needed Immediately

"TIMES" FLOOD RELIEF FUND

The Times will receive, acknowledge by publication and turn over to the proper authorities any contributions sent in care of this paper for the relief of the flood victims of the San Francisquito disaster. The Times announces a contribution of $1000 of its own to start this fund. The need for quick relief is very urgent and all able to do so are urged to subscribe at once and in as large sums as possible. All checks sent to The Times should be made payable to The Times Flood Relief Fund. Receipt is acknowledged of a check for $500 from Anita M. Baldwin. A telegram from Robert J. Foster at Louisville, Ky., states that $100 is being telegraphed by him to this paper for the fund.

Southern California mobilized yesterday on a wide-spreading front for the victims of the St. Francis Dam disaster. Shelter and food for homeless survivors are badly needed. Red Cross chapters of Los Angeles county, and of Ventura and Kern counties, responding quickly to the cry for help, last night had made much headway in the establishment of temporary housing for the hundreds whose homes had been destroyed and in the opening of kitchens for hungry survivors as well as for the hundreds of men employed in rescue work. The Salvation Army also was on hand aiding in the humanitarian work.

Men plowed through mud and debris as rescue work went on in the devastated area. Where once bloomed flowering trees and other vegetation, bodies of those trapped in the rushing wall of water lay exposed on slimy banks. Group here and there struggled through lanes blocked by clogging timbers, uprooted trees and mud-caked debris, pushing and pulling portable camp kitchens in an effort to get warm food to the sufferers, many of whom were stranded and shivering on small shoals in the middle of turbulent streams.

The work of the rescuers was disheartening. Many bodies were buried underneath tightly packed mud. Victims were trapped while they slept, clad only in night clothes. Hurled along on the twisting flood, their bodies were buffeted about making identification in many cases almost impossible. Dance halls, drug stores and almost every available place where rescue work could be conducted were commandeered. First-aid stations and morgues were established in all central points.

RED CROSS ON JOB

Before dawn the local committee of the Red Cross had established headquarters at Newhall where first aid and nursing service from the Los Angeles corps reported for duty. A hundred-bed hospital completely equipped to care for patients was loaded on trucks and reached the Newhall station early yesterday morning.

The Board of Water and Power Commissioners answered the call of the stricken people by appropriating $25,000 for relief work among the sufferers of the flood. The resolution was transmitted to the City Council and approved.

More than 300 members of the Los Angeles Police Department were dispatche by Chief Davis to the areas most seriously affected. All of these men were reported to have reached their destination before noon yesterday. Special details were rushed in fast cars to the stricken country about Saugus and Piru. Squads were deployed down the Santa Clara River co-operating with hundreds of county and State officials and other volunteers.

Members of the American Legion and details of police officers were rushed from Bakersfield to the Saugus district.

Linemen working on the restoration of wires between Saugus and Santa Barbara worked at a frenzied pace and completed their jobs early yesterday morning so that they could volunteer for relief work. More than 500 men left for different parts of the flooded sections to assist Red Cross nurses and doctors in rescue work.

Citizens of Oxnard and Fillmore reported late yesterday afternoon that immediate Red Cross aid is not needed in their districts

(Continued on Page 2, Column 7)

FLOOD AREA IN CONTROL

Army of Deputies Rule Region

Health Crews Working to Prevent Epidemic of Typhoid Fever

Ridge Route Traffic Turned Back at Burbank and North Hollywood

Every available man from the Los Angeles County Sheriff's office, from the County Health Department and from the motorcycle divisions of both Los Angeles and Kern counties and from the State Motor Patrol was dispatched to the scene of the flood during early morning hours yesterday and by nightfall the work of maintaining traffic control and of imposing the stringent sanitary measures deemed necessary was going smoothly but with energy.

Typhoid and contagions often present after flood disasters were being guarded against by the use of antityphoid serum and the enforcement of pure drinking water regulations.

The entire area around the Santa Clara Valley was under semimilitary control by deputy sheriffs, aided by volunteer citizens and members of the American Legion, and no one not included in the great

(Continued on Page 5, Column 3)

PARTIAL LIST OF PERSONS DEAD, INJURED AND MISSING IN FLOOD

The following is a partial and best obtainable list of identified dead, unidentified dead, missing and injured in the St. Francis dam break yesterday.

As well as the below listed persons the authorities are searching for hundreds of missing men, women and children in San Francisquito Canyon, Fillmore, Saugus region, Piru, Ventura, Santa Paula, Castaic, Oberg, Camulos and other sections.

According to figures from improvised morgues in the stricken area and from the Sheriff's office and police department more than 200 bodies of men, women and children have been recovered of which in the neighborhood of seventy-five have been identified.

The Dead

Identified dead at morgue at Newhall:

..Earl Pike.
W. Y. Weinland.
Marion Casper.
Mrs. Ruth Hoppe.
Mrs. Ray Rising.
Mrs. Nell Hanson.
Kenneth Coe.
John Parker.
Dick Pike.
C. J. Mathews, 2 years of age.
Mrs. H. E. Holt.
Sol J. Byrd.
Roland Errarchuo, 14 months.
Three children of Mrs. Ray Rising.
Thelma Mathews.
Vida Mathews.
Mrs. C. J. Mathews.
Eddie Price.
Griffith Hughes.
Rosaria Ruiz.
Mrs. Rosie Errarchuo.
Will W. Nelson, Jr.
Mrs. Nora Coe.
Home Coe.
Eugene Frazier.
Mrs. Rita Kennedy.
May Mathis, 6.
Eugene Kennedy, infant.
Ethel Cochrane.
Francis Garcia.
Tootsie Garcia.
M. J. Garcia.
Joy Hughes.
Alberta Isaac.
Maxie Brosky.
George Mann.
Mrs. Louise Burns.
Margaret Ely.

IDENTIFIED DEAD IN MORGUE AT PIRU:

Edward Locke.

IDENTIFIED DEAD IN MORGUE AT FILLMORE:

Clinton Anderson, foreman, Edison Company.
Keith Anderson.
Ollive Gurcher.
H. Patterson.
Nick Mondlock.
George Berselo.
Mrs. Ethel Boardman.
Mrs. .... Savala.
Mrs. .... Koffer.
Mrs. J. Carrillo.
Eight children of Mrs. J. Carrillo.
M. Miyachi, Japanese.
Mrs. .... Tatley.
Two girls and two boys, children of Charles Rogers.
Oscar Doty.
John Kingston.

Of the above dead, six were employed by the Edison company in a camp near Piru with 150 other men. Eighty of them have been accounted for.

Identified dead in morgue at Santa Paula.

Mrs. S. A. Whitehead.
L. G. Robertson.
Mattillda Samaniego.

Identified dead in morgue at Moorpark.

Elizabeth Torres.
Gordon Cummings.
Mrs. Gordon Cummings.
Bruce Lee.
Mrs. Ida Kelly.
Phillis Kelly, 7.
Delores Kelly, 4.
Mrs. D. Stevens.
Earl Cowden.
Mrs. G. R. Bordman.

Identified dead in morgue at Oxnard:

eff Johnson.

UNIDENTIFIED DEAD:

Newhall, seven.
Fillmore, thirty.
Santa Paula, thirty-two.
Moorpark, nine.
Ventura, seven.

UNACCOUNTED FOR

In and around Santa Paula—One hundred and fifty.

KNOWN INJURED

Selma McCauley, Fillmore. She is in Santa Paula Hospital, not expected to recover from being battered by debris and due to exposure.

C. H. Hunick.
Bernard Ramos.
Miguel Ruiz.
Ceellie Frazer.
Mrs. Lena Fraser.
Charles D. Fraser.
L. R. Ruiz.
Lester Johnson.
Louis Heptins.
John Peiffer.
Curtis Randall.
Albert Davis.
Mrs. Mary Nichols.
Chester Smith.
Mrs. A. L. Garcia.
Benjamin Dornaleche.
Van Dornaleche.
Tenase Ramos.
Mrs. F. Fraser.
L. M. Steenblock, Galt, Iowa.
Everett Goold, Victor, Colo.
L. F. Bennett, Fresno.
"Mazu" Anderson, no address.
H. A. Whitaker, Los Angeles.
E. Gilroy, San Francisco.
William Davis, Los Angeles.
R. G. Barworth, Los Angeles.
Albert M. Hill, Tony, Wyo.
Samuel Ucurso, Visalia, Cal.
Russell Roth, Bakersfield.
J. P. Toomey, Los Angeles.
J. R. Duke, no address.
G. E. Cameron, no address.
C. R. Kerr, Lindsay, Cal.
Peter Bozzite, Los Angeles.
Herbert Anthony, Exeter, Cal. (broken right leg.)
Roy D. Purdy, Sawtelle, Cal.
R. A. Newell, Bakersfield, Cal.
Chris H. Kline, Tulare, Cal.
S. J. Hurst, Maryland.
G. E. Kanawayer, Fresno.
Oliver Crocker, Kansas City.
W. B. Smith, Picayune, Miss.

DEMOCRATS TO HEAR PALMER

William Fleet Palmer, formerly assistant United States Attorney, will be the speaker at the Democratic Luncheon Club tomorrow at the Alexandria. His subject will be "Issues and Leaders of the 1872 Democratic Convention."

The index to today's issue of "The Times" will be found on Page 5, this section.

SCORES MORE THOUGHT BURIED IN DEBRIS OF WILD WATERS

Darkness Halts Rescue as Crews Sight Other Bodies; Hundreds of Homes Crushed by Fatal Torrent and Many Bridges Washed Away

Approximately 200 persons dead, 300 others unaccounted for, and property damage estimated at $7,000,000, according to the latest available figures, is the toll of the disaster following collapse of the St. Francis Dam Monday night which released an avalanche of water upon the sleeping residents of San Francisquito Canyon and the Santa Clara Valley and left death and destruction in its wake.

Of those listed among the missing it is believed by officials engaged in rescue work that many will be found safe. Because of the confusion created by the establishment of morgues at widely separated places it is believed that duplications in the compilation of the number of unidentified dead has taken place.

That the death toll will continue to grow higher, however, was the conclusion of rescue crews who stopped work last night because of darkness and the inaccessibility of many canyons and crevices were other bodies are believed to be lodged.

Many bodies, which could not be taken out last night, were sighted by searchers and will be removed this morning.

FEAR MANY MORE ARE DEAD

Officials in charge of the rescue and body recovering work, last night estimated that probably fifty additional victims at least will be found today.

Property damage throughout the area laid waste by the disaster is estimated at $7,000,000, which is admittedly only a rough guess and it will be several days before an accurate survey can be made.

The magnitude of the sweeping scope of death-dealing torrent that plunged entire families and to their deaths and swept all their possessions away was emphasized in the estimated figures on the number of dwellings destroyed.

Approximately 400 houses located in the San Francisquito Canyon in the sixteen-mile gorge between Piru and the dam site, were wiped out.

Not a standing timber was left as a marker to indicate some once prosperous little farms that dotted the valley.

HOMES NOW MASS OF WRECKAGE

Three hundred houses at Santa Paula, in the southern section of the town, were caught in the flood and swept into a mass of wrecked and tangled timbers as the wall of water rushed from the dam down through the Santa Clara River bed. Thirty or forty houses were wrecked at Fillmore and fifteen at Piru, nine miles south of there.

Al bridges excepting the State highway bridge at Montalvo and the Saticoy bridge were wiped out.

The Los Angeles Bureau of Power and Light suffered the heaviest single loss in the disaster in the St. Francis dam and power plant No. 2, located at the foot of the giant basin. The city's loss will approximate $3,000,000.

The balance of the damage is in the homes and ranches of the San Francisquito Valley and the valley of the Santa Clara River, to which the downrushing flood was diverted near Castaic, in public utility lines destroyed, highways and brindges washed out and live stock drowned.

The loss in the Santa Clara Valley is estimated at more than $3,000,000. A mile of paved highway between Piru and Castaic is washed out. Two of the largest ranches in that district, owned by T. M. Storke, publisher of the Santa Barbara Daily News, and Gwyn Thurmond, were swept by water.

Immense pieces of the dam carried along by the force of the water, were found half a mile and more downstream, according to Lieut. Earl H. Robinson of the National Guard Aero Corps, who made an air survey of San Francisquito Canyon yesterday.

Lieut. Robinson reported that the pumping stations and ranch houses in the path of the flood seem to be wiped out.

The collapse of the dam still is a mystery to the engineers of the Water Bureau who constructed it, and an investigation has been launched to attempt to fix the cause of the tragedy.

William Mulholland, chief engineer of the Water Bureau, ar-

(Continued on Page 2, Column 1)

ENGINEERS FIX BLAME

Dam Break Held Due to Fault

Mountain on West Side Grew Weak and Caused Flood, Mulholland Says

Others State Structure Was Last Word in Project of Gravity Type

The Board of Water and Power Commissioners yesterday started an investigation into the cause of the collapse of the St. Francis Dam and late in the afternoon Chief Engineer Mulholland and Assistant Chief Engineer Van Norman of the water department returned from an all-day visit to the dam and reported to the board. These engineers said the direct, immediate cause of the collapse was the giving way of the mountain on the west side of the canyon.

Due to causes unknown, possibly a fault in the mountain structure or to rains, the mountain on the west side of the dam had become weakened. The west side of the dam was the first to go, and it caused the anchorage of the dam on that side to give way. This was not a part of the dam proper, but a 1500-foot dike or secondary dam which acted as an abutment or anchorage for the main central arch of the dam, which still stands. As the west-side dike gave way, water poured through into the canyon.

On his return from his trip to the scene of the disaster, Chief Engineer Mulholland of the Municipal Water Department issued the following statement:

"I would not venture at this time to express a positive opinion as to the cause of the St. Francis Dam disaster.

"Mr. Van Norman and I arrived

(Continued on Page 6, Column 4)

This was the front page of the *Los Angeles Times* on Wednesday, March 14, 1928, following the St. Francis Dam disaster. (Courtesy of the John Nichols Gallery.)

This was the scene at the Santa Paula Cemetery as the victims were laid to rest. Not all of the victims were buried at the same time, since search teams were still digging out bodies from the mud and debris. (Both, courtesy of the John Nichols Gallery.)

Three

Santa Paula Businesses and the Community

The heart and soul of a community are its businesses, schools, churches, and its traditions. Santa Paula is a very close-knit town, and has been since the beginning. Families help families, businessmen support one another, and high on their priority list are their churches and schools. They manage to keep their traditions alive and work together in camaraderie as they enjoy the festivities, their parades, and fiestas.

The Walnut House was a booming business in Santa Paula. Workers were hired seasonally, and the nuts were shipped to Los Angeles, where they were shelled. In the 1920s, Eugene Kimball designed a dehydrator to dry the walnuts.

Lima Beans were another important product of Santa Paula, as were apricots.

This barn is still standing on the Faulkner farm in Santa Paula. The George Washington Faulkner house was built in 1894.

Mastercraft Laundry was a very important business to the community because it helped launder clothing belonging to the oil field workers, among others.

Charles C. Teague, Wallace Hardison's great-nephew, came to California on his uncle's recommendation. At first, he was disappointed in the small town, but he and his family took on an important role in the community via business and community activities.

The Teague family is featured here. From left to right are (first row, on floor) unidentified, Alan Teague, Judy Teague, Kathleen Cox, and Winifred Cox; (second row, seated) Maiya Teague, Milton Teague, Harriet McKevett Teague, Charles C. Teague, Alice Teague Cox, Charles Teague, and unidentified; (third row, standing) Alfrida Poco Teague, John Cox, and two unidentified.

Congressman Milton Teague was elected to the US House of Representatives and often met with his constituents during their visits to Washington, DC. His assistant was Monty Winkler of Bardsdale.

Charro Marquez was part of the Marquez family, who owned a very popular restaurant and bakery in Santa Paula, the Marquez Bakery. They produced and sold tortillas and other Mexican food as well as pan dulce.

Vesta Fansler was a gifted pianist and was Santa Paula's first female telegrapher in the depot. She married Herman Keene, famed mountain man, lion hunter, and eccentric. Some Fansler family members lived in Santa Paula, and others lived in the neighboring community of Fillmore. One of them married Sally Stanford, the mayor of Sausalito. They were only married for a short time, as Stanford was not accustomed to living in one place for very long. She became restless and moved on without ever saying goodbye.

King & Wood was a photography business purchased from J.C. Brewster. Clarence E. King built a more permanent structure and opened a furniture store. His sons later managed King's Furniture.

Lopez Grocery on 10th Street served many Mexican families in the community. Faustino Lopez, the proprietor, is behind the counter at right with his son José. Another son, Selso, peeks out from behind customer José Quezado.

In 1888, the Bank of Santa Paula was organized by Charles H. McKevett. It became First National Bank of Santa Paula in 1899. The second floor was designed to accommodate the Masonic lodge.

Santa Paula Police Department and city staff members are seen in this photograph. From left to right are (first row) Erbie Wilson, unidentified, fire chief Sam Primmer, Barbara Mosher Harrington, Tess Price, and ? Rhodes; (second row) Bob Crumline, Frank Engledow, Horace Dowell, Grant Mickel, police captain Tom Moore, and unidentified; (third row) Edith Fandre, Thelma Minor, Agnes ?, Judge Alice McGill, unidentified, and Deputy Perry Barker.

The Santa Paula Fire Department is seen here in 1943 during World War II. They wear their civil defense helmets and fire gear. From left to right are (first row, kneeling) N.K. Lincoln, Frank Mosher, unidentified, and Leonard Phinney; (second row, standing) Joe Wellman, Herman Rounds, G.A. Giacomazzi, Steve Love, George Harding, Everett Morrison, Chief Warren King, Jack Singleton, and Norman Lair.

The downtown fire station was the first station of its kind in Ventura County. It was built adjoining the county agricultural commissioner's office at the corner of Santa Barbara and Eighth Streets. After a few years, other communities followed suit and built fire stations in various locales.

Del King gas station is seen here in 1940 as it looked during the 50th-year celebration of the founding of the Union Oil Company of California in Santa Paula. The company was founded by Wallace Hardison and Lyman Smith. It was a full-service station, where it was customary for the workers to wash the windows and check the oil and tire pressure in addition to filling the tanks with gasoline.

The *Santa Paula Chronicle* staff are featured here in front of the newspaper building. The *Chronicle* has served the community for over 100 years. The Blanchard Community Library and the Santa Paula Historical Society digitized many years of articles and photographs for their archives. In 1993, the paper changed its name to the *Santa Paula Times* and was owned by Don and Debbie Johnson for a number of years. Today, the *Times* is owned by editor and publisher Peggy Kelly.

The Glen Tavern Inn is one of Santa Paula's gems, as it is a historical landmark and is part of the permanent fabric of Santa Paula's history. The building was listed in the National Register of Historic Places in 1984, and is an official landmark of Santa Paula and Ventura County. It was built in 1911 as a bungalow in the Craftsman and Tudor Revival styles. In keeping with the hotel's motto, "Where the Past Comes to Life," the inn is allegedly haunted. The Ventura Paranormal Society held its annual convention here in 2007, and it has been featured in *Ghost Adventures* and *The Dead Files*.

The Glen City Theatre burned on a night in December 1949. It had opened in 1919 and was beautifully decorated with grey walls and delicate frescos with landscapes. The theater was an instant sensation in the community.

The Fox West Coast Theater's grand opening on October 12, 1950, was publicized by the *Santa Paula Chronicle*. The theater was the first with air conditioning, and held 1,000 seats, all with padded backs.

This image was captured during Jue's Superette grand opening. Jake Jue and his wife, Mae Soo Hoo, are seen in this photograph on this very exciting day.

Watkins Hardware relocated to Main Street in order to better serve its customers. It provided items for young people as well as for adults. Bob Watkins kept the store in business for a number of years.

Chambers Market, featured here in the early 1950s, was owned by Russ Chambers since 1938. He maintained the grocery department and leased out the meat and liquor departments. It was housed in the Balcom Hall building, but in the early 1960s, the market burned down under suspicious circumstances.

Roy Wilson Sr. was a well-known architect in Santa Paula. He designed the Isbell School, H.B. Skillen Mortuary, and more.

Ralph Dickenson and Dan Emmet purchased land near the Santa Clara River south of Santa Paula for an airport. After several months of construction, the new Santa Paula Airport opened to the public in 1930. Steve McQueen frequented the airport when he lived in Santa Paula.

From high above, this view shows what the Santa Paula Airport looked like in the 1960s. Much of the original 1930s-era facilities still exist today.

Harold Michel received his pilot's license from the Santa Paula Airport and its aviation department. He housed his plane in one of the hangars there and flew as often as he could. Many in Ventura County have received their aviation license from the Santa Paula Airport's C.P. Aviation Flight School.

Pete Romero served in World War II as a staff sergeant in the 145th Infantry Regiment of the 37th Division and was a squad leader in the Pacific. He was awarded numerous medals, including two Purple Hearts.

Blaine Romney received his law degree from George Washington University. He enlisted in the Air Force and served as a major. He married Jeanette Hardison, and in 1946 was appointed the city attorney for Santa Paula.

Richard Cummings served during World War II and joined the US Army Air Corps at Luke Army Air Base in Arizona. Lieutenant Cummings served as a flight instructor, although he was trained as a fighter pilot. His aerial classroom was the AT-6 Texan, which could maneuver very well. A majority of the Allied pilots trained on the Texan.

Donald Jue was stationed in the Philippines during World War II. He served as an ambulance driver, and managed the post's grocery store.

Jess Victoria was an infantry medic with the 123rd Regiment in the Pacific Theater. Corporal Victoria was awarded the Bronze Star for running through enemy fire to save a fellow soldier.

Robert Fogata served in Europe during World War II in the US Army. He served in France in 1943 prior to the Normandy invasion. He was present in Rome in June 1944 when General Patton's Third Army tanks entered the city.

Joe Villa II served in the US Army during World War II. His brother Herman Villa served in the Korean War and was killed in action in June 1952.

Col. Doug Shively married Lucy Smith, an accomplished concert pianist. He is one of Santa Paula's illustrious artists and became the president of Citizens State Bank.

Sing Hing and his family are pictured here. They carried the valuable china shown below from China to Santa Paula more than 100 years ago. Sing Hing gave the china to Nathan Weston Blanchard in exchange for housing. The family worked for the Blanchards. (Courtesy of the Betsy Blanchard Chess family.)

This is the china Sing Hing carried to Santa Paula from his homeland. The two photographs on this page are part of the Smithsonian traveling exhibition I Want the Wide American Earth. It is part of the Asian Pacific American Experience and the Museum of American History at the Smithsonian Institution. (Courtesy of the Betsy Blanchard Chess family.)

The Hardison family followed their many relatives to California and continued to prosper in the Ventura County area.

Ruth and Wallace Hardison were the children of A.C. and Cora Hardison. Robert Hardison served four years in the US Army Air Corps during World War II.

Mary Thille donated the money to help complete the building of the Guadalupe Roman Catholic Church on the east side of Santa Paula. The Thille family were very generous philanthropists, and it was Albert and Grace Thille who donated the initial funds to build Santa Paula Memorial Hospital.

The Limoneira Japanese Picnic is seen here The Japanese workers lived in one area of the ranch, with the Mexicans and others in their own areas.

Leon Preciado (far left) is pictured with his fellow carpenters at the Blanchard packing plant in 1909. These men made citrus crates from pine or fir. The crates seen here carry Lemon Spray brand labels.

Santa Paula Birth Hospital is where mothers from Santa Paula, Fillmore, and the Piru area gave birth. Today's baby boomers in the Santa Paula area can attest to having been born there.

The Cub Scouts of 1948 were very active in the community.

Bank of America's original location is seen here; today, it is across from the Santa Paula Theatre Center. In this photograph, it is across from the Citizen's State Bank. The Bank of America of California merged with the Bank of Italy.

La Hacienda on East Main Street served Mexican food. The owner, Ruby Dominguez Carrillo Cardenas, poses here in front of her café.

Victoria Shoe Repair was owned by Manuel Victoria. He and his brother Salvador served the public from a corner room in the Union Oil Building on Main Street downtown. Later, Manuel resumed the repair shop with his son Jess. Manuel also opened a shoe repair shop in Fillmore.

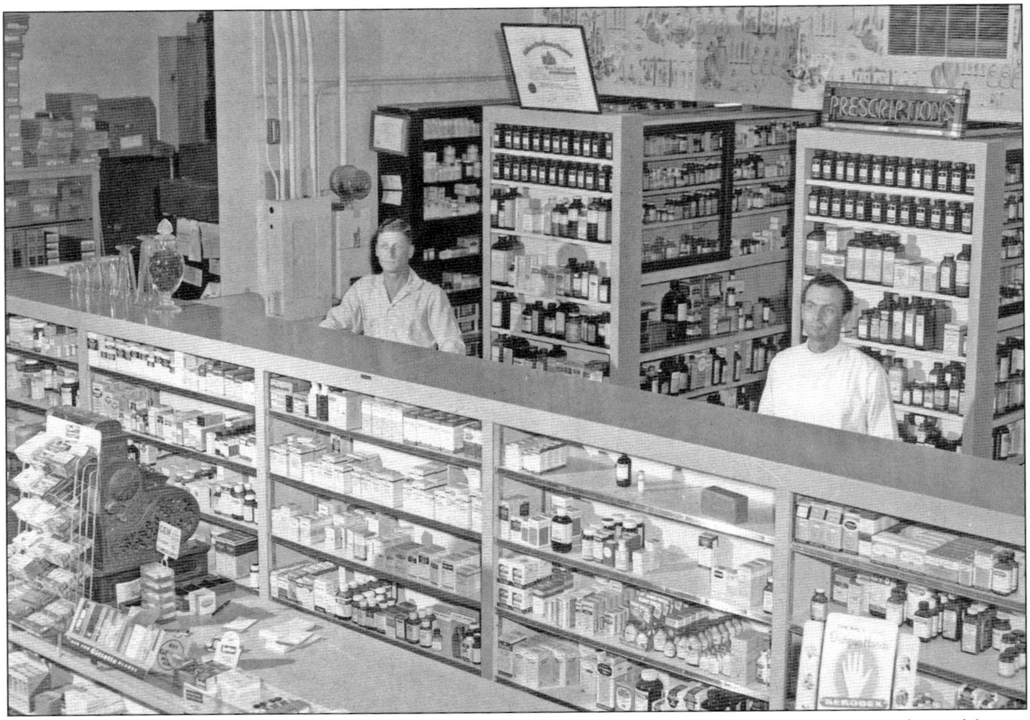

Cauch's Drug Store was purchased by Harold Ringle in 1946. He kept the name since it had been a community staple since the 1880s. Shown here are the two pharmacists, Art Stopey (left) and Walter Pendleton. Cauch's later included more than just pharmacy needs; the shop sold small gifts and ice cream as well as other items.

The Santa Paula Freeway was a major step in transportation advancement. This photograph shows Miss Ventura County, Cindy Stocker of Fillmore, with Priscilla Pritchard, riding in a car during the opening of the freeway.

Dick's Sandwich Shop was known for serving the best chili and beans. Standing behind the counter are Gail Deaver and Dick Richey. The shop was owned by Dick Dunbar.

The former South Grammar School had six classrooms. The principal was David Reese, and the teachers were Jessie Clark, Carrie Fleisher, Mr. Kyle, and Jessie Todd. The building is now city hall.

The Methodist church young men's group shown here is an example of one of the activities available to the young people of Santa Paula in the 1940s.

Pastor Luis Tirre of El Buen Pastor organized a youth group each year that he served at the Spanish Community Missionary Church.

Casa del Mexicano was established in Los Angeles in 1931, and the founding members of the Santa Paula Casa del Mexicano are featured here. From left to right are (first row) Juan Ruiz, unidentified, Andrea Mendoza, Al Pienada, Juan Salas, Jose Diaz, and four unidentified; (second row) Lorenzo Avina, Toni Salas, Estella Salas, Juana Marquez, Camen Arguelles, three unidentified, Josefa Diaz, and four unidentified; (third row) Ysmael Gonzales, Maxine Gonzales, Maria Avina, eight unidentified, Nomie Salas, Virginia Marquez, Estella Escobedo, Concepción Salas, and Tommie Solis. The rest are unidentified. The Casa del Mexicano is still active today and serves the needs of the Hispanic community through community and civic activities.

Barbara Webster School changed its name from Canyon School to honor principal Barbara Webster, seen here at far right in 1942. It was one of the first schools built in Santa Paula and provided classes from kindergarten through eighth grade.

Bernice King's Glen City School class is pictured here in 1960. The school is on the west side of town and used to house an old Air Force plane on its playground, where children could climb and play.

The Isbell School, seen here in the 1930s, is an icon in Santa Paula. It was designed by architect Roy Wilson Sr., and the school was named for Isbell Olive Mann, the first teacher in California. The school was dedicated in 1926; two years later, the St. Francis Dam disaster flooded the first floor with mud and debris. The school was cleaned and refurbished and is still in use today.

Helen Soto is pictured at right front getting ready to tend the garden at Olivelands School. The older students at Olivelands kept this garden as they learned about plants and gardening during the school year.

Santa Paula High School has been depicted in numerous films, including *Carrie*.

El Solano is the yearbook for Santa Paula High School. The 1935 staff seen here received an honor in the yearly All-American Yearbook Competition. Having received 865 points out of a possible 1,000, their dedication and skills were recognized and honored.

Helen Jue (left) and Irene Alvarez are seen here prior to their 1959 graduation at Santa Paula High School.

The Santa Paula High School Band was a favorite at football games and other community festivities and parades.

Harvesting of apricots and walnuts continued during World War II, with the work being done by Santa Paula High School students. They were excused at midday to go to work.

Don Dickenson, seen here in 1940, is an example of the many students who played football at Ventura County schools. The rivalry between Santa Paula and Fillmore is the oldest between schools in Southern California. Since the games started in 1924, the Santa Paula Cardinals and the Fillmore Flashes have played every year except 1942 because of World War II, 1969 due to being in separate leagues, and 2019, when their game was canceled due to the Maria Fire, but they intend to make up for that missed game at their next matchup. Santa Paula leads the series with 61 wins to Fillmore's 40. They have tied seven times.

Four

Early History and Pioneers in Fillmore

The best way to tell a story is visually. With a photograph, a flood of memories may be conjured up. The images take on a life of their own for each individual. Many of the descendants of the pioneer families still have a connection to Fillmore and Bardsdale. They reside in the community or return for special events and celebrations. Growing up in Fillmore, Bardsdale, and Piru, everyone knew everyone else and whose families children belonged to. It was a time when everyone watched over everybody else, especially the children. If one got into trouble at school, whether it be a little skirmish or not finishing homework, their parents knew about it before they arrived home, and there were consequences. Neighbors helped one another, and there was a camaraderie of spirit that is unique to small communities. It all started with the era of the Californios and the purchase of property, as T. Wallace More and his brothers did. The city of Fillmore was named for Jerome P. Fillmore, the general superintendent of the Southern Pacific Railroad. The railroad came through in 1887–1888, and the town was established in 1888 and incorporated in 1914. The community is diverse, with various cultures living together in harmony.

In 1829, Don Carlos Antonio Carrillo, a resident of Santa Barbara, petitioned the provincial governor of Alta California for the tract of land known as Rancho Sespe. Not until Gen. Jose Figueroa became governor in 1833 did he confirm this and grant the concession. No grant was made for less than one square league, or approximately 4,428 acres. At this point, there is confusion because the file relating to the concession contains two copies of the official grant. Both have the same date of May 29, 1834, and both are signed by Governor Figueroa and the secretary, Augustin Zamorano. Both list the conditions of the concession, that Carrillo must build a house and get the property surveyed. One states the grant is for two leagues, but the other lists six leagues.

On February 2, 1848, the United States acquired California under the terms of the Treaty of Guadalupe Hidalgo. Then gold was discovered in northern California, and gold-seekers passed through the Santa Clara River Valley on their way to seek their fortunes.

Scores of families faced economic ruin. Don Carlos Carrillo died in 1852, and his widow passed away a year later in February 1853. Then, in April 1853, the land commission confirmed the original petition of Carlos Antonio for Rancho Sespe. It was approved for six leagues, or 26,000 acres. A few months after this decision, the probate court of Santa Barbara ordered the estate held by Josefa Carrillo to be sold at auction.

T. Wallace More purchased six leagues of Rancho Sespe at the Santa Barbara auction. His two brothers joined him raising cattle and sheep. There was a dispute as to how many acres he had actually purchased because he thought he had purchased the full six leagues, but the courts decided he had bought only two. More was at odds with those who began homesteading on acreage he believed to be in the public domain. On the night of March 24, 1877, More was shot and killed on his ranch while trying to put out a fire in his barn, which had been deliberately set by the men who shot him.

Susannah More de Ortega from Santa Barbara was the wife of T. Wallace More. More had been disliked by most of the settlers in the area, which resulted in a slow and ineffective investigation into his murder. Eventually, seven were indicted: J.S Churchill, John Curlee, W.H. Hunt, Jesse Jones, J.D. Lord, Charles McCart, and Frank Sprague. Curlee was found guilty but later won a new trial and was acquitted. Sprague was found guilty and sentenced to death, but after serving seven years in San Quentin, he was pardoned by the governor and released. Susannah More passed away two years after her husband's murder.

In 1888, financier Morton Hull of Chicago foreclosed on Rancho Sespe after the death of Susannah More de Ortega. In 1895, he gave half of the property to his daughter Eudora and the other half to her twin brother Morton. Eudora was married to Keith Spalding, son of Albert G. Spalding, who transformed the game of baseball into a professional sport and founded the Spalding Sporting Goods company. Eudora and Keith Spalding, pictured here, made Rancho Sespe a successful working ranch in the early 20th century. They enjoyed the outdoors and traveling the world. (Courtesy of Fillmore Historical Society.)

In this view of the valley, San Cayetano Mountain is seen in the background. W.H. Fleet was hired by Keith Spalding in May 1910 as the first manager of Rancho Sespe. It was Fleet who had the lemon-packing plant built alongside the Southern Pacific Railroad at Highway 126 and Telegraph Road. He was the overseer of the bunkhouses, and built homes for the staff and for workers' families. As acreage for the fruit orchards increased, so did the labor force, and Fleet had more homes built to accommodate them.

The Rancho Sespe bunkhouse seen here is now home to the Fillmore Historical Museum. This was officially the No. 2 bunkhouse. The No. 1 bunkhouse was designed by Green and Green of Pasadena. (Courtesy of the Ybarra family.)

More housing was built during the 1920s and 1930s due to an increase in fruit production. Sespe Village had 140 single-family homes, a store, and a recreation building, or dance hall, as many remember it. The community held many celebrations and dances there. School was held at San Cayetano School, north of Sespe Village, and the children would walk there. Later, a school from Kindergarten to third grade was available in Sespe Village, and buses would transport the older children to Fillmore schools.

Abundio Delgado Sanchez and Concepción "Concha" Guzman Nieves were born in Silao, Guanajuato, Mexico. They had five children: Lupe, Carlos, Dolores, Soledad, and Arnulfo. They left Mexico for Riverside, California, where Abundio's cousin Pedro Romero had said he would help Abundio find a job. In the early 1920s, Abundio built the Sanchez Brothers Mexican Mercantile, which still stands on the corner of Main and Mountain View Streets. The Sanchez Mercantile was successful for eight years until the Depression. The family extended credit to their customers, which put them out of business. Abundio sold the business to Jose Gonzalez and his wife, Jesse. (Courtesy of the Mary Ramirez family.)

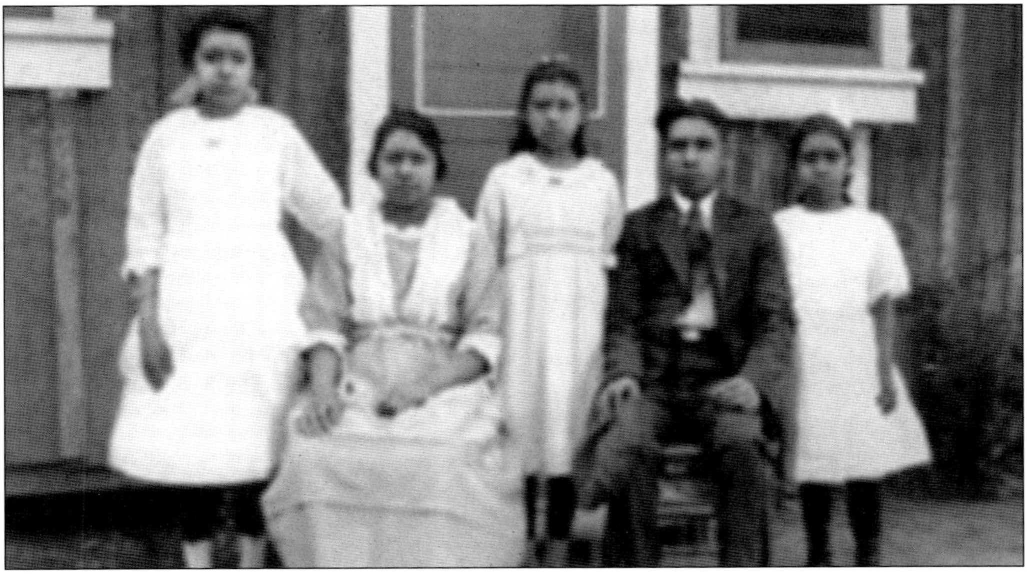

The Sanchez children are pictured here. From left to right are Refugio, Soledad, Guadalupe, Arnulfo, and Maria. After Abundio sold the market, Concepción and her children made corn tortillas out of their home using a tortilla press. Later, Mary was born, followed by Ruth. The older children went door-to-door, taking orders and delivering tortillas. They earned enough money to put food on the table and help pay monthly expenses. Arnulfo purchased his own market in Piru in the 1950s, and it remained in the family. His son Jimmy and his wife, Lucy, later managed the market. (Courtesy of Mary Ramirez family.)

The Smithsonian Institution's Museum of American History features an exhibit called Food: Transforming the American Table 1950–2000, The Mexican Food Revolution. Included in the exhibit is the tortilla press used by the Concepción Sanchez family. (Courtesy of the Division of Cultural and Community Life, National Museum of American History, Smithsonian Institution.)

Concepción Sanchez used this electric *molino* to make corn tortillas. She made large quantities, and had enough left over on the weekends to sell to the neighbors. She also sold them through her son Arnulfo's store. (Courtesy of the Division of Cultural and Community Life, National Museum of American History, Smithsonian Institution.)

This tortilla press held the cornmeal, or *masa*, to make corn tortillas. The press would mash the masa and shape it into round tortillas. Concha also used the masa to produce tamales, a Mexican favorite, especially around Christmastime. (Courtesy of the Division of Cultural and Community Life, National Museum of American History, Smithsonian Institution.)

Concepción Sanchez's apron is on display at the Smithsonian Institution's Museum of American History. (Courtesy of Division of Cultural and Community Life, National Museum of American History, Smithsonian Institution.)

Irene Gonzalez (left) and her daughter Linda Gonzalez Godoy are pictured here. Irene used to help Jesse Gonzalez (no relation) at her store after Jesse's husband passed away during the late 1930s. She also helped Concha Sanchez make tortillas, and helped sell them in the neighborhood. (Author's collection.)

Concepción Sanchez's daughter Soledad Sanchez Ybarra is pictured with two of her many great-grandchildren. She is celebrating the birth of Elizabeth's new little brother, Robert. (Author's collection.)

At left are, from left to right, Donna and Dr. Richard "Ricky" Ramirez and his mother, Mary Ramirez. At right is Anna Ríos Bermudez, Concepción Sanchez's granddaughter and curator of collections at the Museum of Ventura County. Dr. Ramirez is a guidance counselor at American River College, and grew up in Fillmore. (Author's collection.)

Germán and Maria Romero lived in Fillmore for many years and had 17 children. They instilled a strong work ethic in all their children, who attended colleges throughout the United States.

The Romero family is pictured during a family picnic. The Romero children grew up to be successful professionals including nurses, teachers, principals, and managers; one became a nun in a convent, and another an airline stewardess.

Julius Balden arrived in the Fillmore-Bardsdale area in 1891. He had two sons, Harold and Lloyd. The Balden family helped shape the community of Fillmore, as they owned land in the area and sold it for development and to local businesses.

Harold Balden is pictured here with Fillmore High School classmates behind the "2" in 1921. He and his wife, Mary, built their home on the corner of Second and Saratoga Streets. Balden managed the family business, Balden Ranching Company, along with the family's citrus orchards.

In 1861, O.J. Goodenough enlisted in the Union army and was a wagon master from 1862 to 1863. He moved to Fillmore, where he farmed from 1883 until his death in 1895. He built the first school in Bardsdale and was one of the founders of the Fillmore Presbyterian Church. He married Zedora Tietsort and they had five children. Two of them are shown here.

Otto Jones owned the Jones Brothers gas station, later Jones Brothers and Sons. In the early morning after the St. Francis Dam disaster, he and his pregnant wife opened the station for customers. Their children Laurabelle and Stan are seen here.

From left to right, Carole Shiells, Eddie Ybarra, and Lynda Edmunds are seen at a Fillmore High School alumni dinner.

Sharon and Dave Villasenor are one of Fillmore's first couples. They have remained active in community activities as well as philanthropic causes. Dave's father, Herky Villasenor, served lunches and dinners to the Mexican farmworkers who tended the citrus crops in Fillmore.

Jack Starnes showcases the Sanitary Dairy truck during the Fillmore Festival parade. Russell Hardison acquired the dairy after he returned from service in World War II and ran it until 1977.

William Shiells married Sarah Thompson in 1893. He was a director of the Fillmore State Bank and in 1914 was elected to the Ventura County board of supervisors. The Shiells family is seen here on vacation in their new Cadillac. The children in back are Helen, James Francis, William Jr., and Lester.

Five

Rancho Sespe and Bardsdale

Living in the Heritage Valley offers many unique opportunities for exploring the local history of the community and the historical landmarks that enrich the region. There is a sense of camaraderie in business, and the attitude of helping one another is significant. The William L. Morris car dealership has been in Fillmore since 1929, when William L. Morris Sr. opened his first dealership in Fillmore. The dealership passed to William L. Morris Jr., and eventually, grandson Jeff Morris opened a dealership in Simi Valley in 1977. Congressman Elton Gallegly presented William L. Morris Jr. with an award for his commitment to the community. Another well-known business that remains is Patterson Hardware. Others that have been part of the fabric of the community are Clough's Drug Store, Jessie's Place, Ballard Furniture, Crawford's Furniture, Ms. Harmonson's fabric store, Ramona Savings, and many more. Traditions still abound, such as the Fillmore May Festival and the July Fourth celebrations, when fireworks are sold to assist nonprofits and church communities. Many descendants still live in Bardsdale and the Fillmore area. Elizabeth Munger Blanchard grew up in the Fillmore-Bardsdale area before she and her family moved to Santa Paula. They are related to the Wileman family, who also cultivated citrus crops.

Brothers John and Manuel Indadomi arrived in Ventura County and started working for the Limoneira Company in Santa Paula, where they picked fruit. They saved their money and purchased a grocery store in Fillmore around 1933, which became Jonson's Market on Main Street. John Inadomi, seen here with his wife, Anna, remained in Fillmore with his family while Manuel moved his family to Oxnard to open another store. During World War II, both Indadomi families were taken to detention camps, leaving almost everything behind. Richard Gonzalez Sr. kept Jonson's Market running until John Inadomi returned. The family relocated to the Los Angeles area, where they opened Jonson's Market in Torrance, California. (Courtesy of the George and Jeannette Inadomi family.)

Fillmore Fish Hatchery is still in use today as a well-organized research facility. (Courtesy of the Minnie Ybarra family.)

Keith and Eudora Spalding had the goal of building Rancho Sespe as a showplace where successful citrus ranching could prosper. Sparing no expense, they hired the Pasadena architectural firm of Green and Green to design the famous Rancho Sespe Bunkhouse, which housed single white men who worked in their citrus orchards. Keith's father was Albert Spalding (pictured), who revolutionized the game of baseball. (Author's collection.)

Ernie and Becky Morales, pictured here at left with Martha Brown, have remained active in the Fillmore community for a number of years. Ernie has served as Fillmore city councilman and as mayor of the city of Fillmore. (Courtesy of the Bob and Diana Cox family.)

The Bardsdale Methodist Church was built in 1898. Thomas Bard donated two lots for its construction and also donated the stained glass windows. The church is still in use today. (Courtesy of the Harold Michel family.)

Monty and Maio Winkler are longtime residents of Bardsdale. Monty served as assistant to Congressman Teague in Washington, DC, in the 1960s. Today, the couple enjoys growing avocados and citrus fruits on their ranch. (Author's collection.)

Harold Michel and his wife, Bernice, settled in Bardsdale. He is a descendent of Jacob Michel. They lived in the family home, and Harold took care of his citrus orchards. (Courtesy of the Michel family.)

Josephine "Jo" Schleimer married Aaron Myers. She grew up in Bardsdale and recalls how she and her brothers would ride their horses to Fillmore by way of A Street, tie up, and go into town. On the night of the St. Francis Dam disaster, her entire family was out of town, saving their lives. Upon their return, there were bodies stuck in trees, and mud was everywhere. (Courtesy of the Bob and Diana Cox family.)

Jack and Jim Schleimer are Josephine Myers's brothers. They grew up in the Bardsdale area as well. (Courtesy of the Bob and Diana Cox family.)

The Bardsdale Post Office was quite small because the community was smaller than most. Royce Surdam served as the first postmaster in the Bardsdale area. (Courtesy of Robert Ybarra.)

These women are the descendants of pioneers of Bardsdale and Fillmore. (Author's collection.)

From left to right are (first row) Robert and Evelynn Grosfield and Barbara and Ernie Leija; (second row) Laura and Robert Ybarra Jr., Elizabeth Blanchard, and Minnie (Herrera) and Woody Ybarra. Minnie Herrera lived with Elizabeth Blanchard and her family as a foster child during her high school years. (Courtesy of the Minnie Ybarra family.)

Farmers worked their fields with either horses or mules. Some families still keep a team of horses on their ranches for hayrides and to show their grandchildren what life used to be like. (Courtesy of the John Nichols Gallery.)

Six

Fillmore Community and Traditions

The city of Fillmore was named after Jerome P. Fillmore, who was the general superintendent of the Southern Pacific Railroad. The railroad came through in 1887–1888, and the town was established in 1888 and incorporated in 1914. The community of Fillmore is diverse, with many Hispanics and Anglos living in harmony.

Fillmore notables are seen here in the 1960s. From left to right are Chief Earl Hume; Councilmen Loren Briggs, Bert Major, Fred Bryce, and Ray Lindenfeld; and Mayor Robert Linville. At this time, Chief Hume was the longest-serving police chief in the United States. He always found the time to keep young people from getting into trouble, calling parents and assisting them in dealing with issues. Sometimes, he had high school kids wash police cars after school. (Courtesy of the Michel family.)

From left to right, Sandy Warring, Mary Blodgett Shiells, and Diana Nichols Cox all graduated from Fillmore High School, and they still find the time to attend the Fillmore alumni dinners. They were very active in school and community activities and remain so today. (Courtesy of the Bob and Diana Cox family.)

Fillmore's population was 150 in 1900, and businesses included a rooming house, general store, pool hall, barbershop, fruit stand, saloon, and lumber yard. Central Avenue, seen here, was filled with people on Saturdays. (Courtesy of the John Nichols Gallery.)

The Fillmore Towne Theatre was built in 1916 and remained in business until 1994. The single-screen theater was segregated from the 1920s to the 1940s, with Mexicans only allowed to sit on the right. This changed after World War II. (Courtesy of the John Nichols Gallery.)

Fillmore State Bank, Fillmore's first bank, opened in 1905 and still stands on Central Avenue. (Courtesy of the John Nichols Gallery.)

William Froehlich's blacksmith shop was a necessity in the community. There was also a livery nearby. (Courtesy of the John Nichols Gallery.)

The Fillmore Pool Hall was owned by K.D. Rogers for years, and was a popular spot for the high school boys to hang out with their friends. It was well known that the pool hall served the best cherry Cokes in town. (Courtesy of the John Nichols Gallery.)

Harvey Patterson owned Patterson's Hardware store in Fillmore, which is still in business today. Since Harvey passed away, his daughter Michele and wife, Emma, have run the store. (Author's collection.)

From left to right, Emma Patterson, Diana Nichols Cox, and Michele Patterson are enjoying a Fillmore alumni dinner. Emma and Michelle Patterson own Patterson Hardware, which was run for many years by Harvey Patterson. (Courtesy of the Bob and Diana Cox family.)

The Fillmore Parade is an annual tradition that is a means for the community to come together. It is usually held in May in conjunction with the Fillmore Festival. Food booths and carnival rides come to town, and everyone celebrates and has a good time. (Courtesy of the John Nichols Gallery.)

Richard Gonzalez's Market in Fillmore was a family business. His mother opened the store, and Irene (Sanchez) Gonzalez helped her during the Depression. After Mrs. Gonzalez passed away, Richard Gonzalez took over the business. (Courtesy of the Richard Gonzalez family.)

Fillmore High School's baseball team was coached by Harry Bigger. The team won many games when Woody Ybarra was the pitcher. (Courtesy of the Ernie Morales family.)

Woody Ybarra served in the US Army during World War II as a sergeant. He was sent with a small team to the perimeter of their encampment on the island of Okinawa to listen to the aircraft flying overhead and report back on the number of enemy planes. He returned to Fillmore and married Minnie Herrera, and they had three children. (Courtesy of the Minnie Ybarra family.)

Brandon Ybarra served in the armed forces and remains a pilot today. (Courtesy of the Minnie Ybarra family.)

Patrick McKinley served in the US Marines. (Courtesy of the Shelley Ybarra McKinley family.)

The Lopez boys valiantly served in the US armed forces. Their mother proudly displays their photographs on her wall at the family business, Vintage Pleasures in Fillmore. (Courtesy of the Lopez family.)

Kevin Monahan, an Air Force pilot, served his country as well. His grandmother Mary Helen Ybarra Monahan grew up in Fillmore and graduated from Fillmore High School. (Courtesy of the Ybarra family.)

This image was captured on moving day in 1958 from the Mountain View School to the brand-new San Cayetano School just up the street.

The old San Cayetano School is seen here when it was situated near Rancho Sespe on the outskirts of Fillmore, on the west side of town. (Author's collection.)

Old Rancho Sespe is seen here in the early 1920s. It served as a schoolhouse for kindergarten through second grade.

Mary Galvin and chancellor Dr. Dorothy Wilson (pictured) are both educators who dedicated their lives to making life better for all young people. Galvin was a kindergarten teacher at Olivelands School for many years in the late 1920s and 1930s, and then taught in the Fillmore Schools. Woody Ybarra had Mary Galvin as his kindergarten teacher at Olivelands, and years later, his daughter Barbara (Ybarra) Leija had Galvin as her kindergarten teacher at Sespe School in Fillmore. Dr. Dorothy Wilson graduated from Fillmore High School and earned her doctorate from Purdue University. She was appointed chancellor of the University of California, Merced, where she is today. (Courtesy of the Ybarra family.)

Seven

Piru and Rancho Camulos

Piru is a small, unincorporated community with a population of 2,083 and a rich history dating to the 1800s. Although it is a small community, Piru is steeped in history, and many of the residents are descendants of the first families of Rancho Camulos. Their ancestors lived on Rancho Camulos or worked for the Del Valle family. The name comes from the Tataviam Indian word for the tule reeds that grow along Piru Creek. These reeds were used by the Tataviam people to weave baskets for carrying and for cooking. Piru was founded in 1887 by David C. Cook, a publisher of Sunday school books and supplies from Illinois. He purchased the Temescal Mexican land grant from the sons of Ygnacio Del Valle and built his first home on the corner of Main and Center Streets. In 1890, he built his permanent home, the lavish Queen Anne–style mansion known as the Piru Mansion. Lake Piru is the recreational area behind the community, and many go boating there and enjoy the picnic areas with their families. Besides the Del Valle family, the Hugh Warring, Chester Warring, Harry Lechler, Donna Chessani, Jose Nunez, Alcocer, Aguirre, and Dominguez families left a lasting impression upon Piru.

Frank Bowdie was Piru's fire chief in 1928 when the district took charge of the Piru Fire Department. In 1931, a fire house was built on Market Street that was in use until 1950. Today, it is on Church Street. (Courtesy of Missy Pennington Cervantez family.)

The Piru Mansion was accidentally burned down during remodeling, and was rebuilt as an exact replica of the original. The owners utilized all the photographs Philip Hardison had taken of the house for a college project.

The Del Valle children pictured here are, from left to right, (first row, seated) Josefa R. (Del Valle) De Forster and Sen. Reginald Del Valle; (second row, standing) Ignacio Del Valle Jr., Ysabel (Del Valle) Cram, and Ulpiano Del Valle. (Courtesy of the Rancho Camulos Museum.)

The Del Valle family is seen on their back stairs at Rancho Camulos. All 48,612 acres of Rancho San Francisco were granted to Antonio Del Valle in 1839 by Gov. Juan B. Alvarado as a reward for Del Valle's exemplary military service. Rancho San Francisco runs from Valencia to Piru. Two years after Antonio's death, the property was divided among his second wife, Jacoba, and the children from his two marriages. His eldest son, Ygnacio, inherited a portion of the ranch where he built a four-room adobe in 1853 at Camulos, on the western boundary of the 1,800 acres he inherited. He stocked the ranch with cattle, fruit and walnut trees, and grapevines. Today, the Camulos Adobe is a state historical landmark. (Courtesy of the Rancho Camulos Museum.)

Reynaldo "Reginald" Del Valle was elected to the state assembly in 1880 and then served as a state senator from 1882 to 1886. A bilingual, bicultural Los Angeles native of Mexican origin, Del Valle was responsible for the establishment and funding of the Los Angeles Normal School, absorbed by the University of California in 1919 to become the University of California, Los Angeles. The original school still stands at Fifth Street and Grand Avenue, the site of the current Los Angeles Public Library. Del Valle invited his friend Charles Lummis to stay at Rancho Camulos to recuperate from a mild stroke, and their friendship lasted until their death. (Courtesy of the Rancho Camulos Museum.)

Charles Lummis was a pioneer photojournalist and the first city editor of the *Los Angeles Times*. While he stayed at Rancho Camulos, he took numerous photographs of the Del Valle sisters and fell in love with Susanita Del Valle, who was 15 at the time. Lummis promised to divorce his wife, but Susanita's grandmother Ysabel Del Valle would not allow the relationship to move forward. Lummis presented Susanita with an album of 83 photographs of her and her sisters and of daily life at Rancho Camulos. The album is part of the Huntington Library collection. Lummis is pictured here with, from left to right, Nena, Enedina, Ysabel, and Susanita Del Valle. (Courtesy of the Rancho Camulos Museum.)

Charles Lummis is pictured at the Rancho Camulos fountain with, from left to right, Nena, Ysabel, and Susanita Del Valle. During his many visits to Rancho Camulos, Lummis made wax recordings of the Del Valle girls singing and playing the guitar. His recordings are now housed in the Braun Research Library collection of the Autry National Center in Los Angeles. (Courtesy of the Huntington Library, San Marino, California.)

D.W. Griffith, the famous Hollywood director, took Mary Pickford to Rancho Camulos, where she starred in the film *Ramona*. In this 1910 photograph, Pickford is at center in front of the Piru Mountain View Hotel. *Ramona* was the first film shot in the Santa Clarita Valley. The hotel was built by Piru founder David Caleb Cook during the early 1870s. (Courtesy of the Rancho Camulos Museum.)

This is the famous chapel at Rancho Camulos. The Franciscan priests came and celebrated Mass once a month, before the town of Piru had built a Roman Catholic church. During these monthly visits, the priests joined in the family celebrations, culminating with food and wine. The priests always tried to convert the local Indian population to Christianity. (Courtesy of the Rancho Camulos Museum.)

Ofelia Sanchez Haynes is the daughter of Ruth Sanchez, the youngest child of Abundio and Concepción Sanchez. She is pictured here with Joe Aguirre. (Courtesy of the Bob and Diana Cox family.)

August Rubel, seen here with his family at Rancho Camulos, first purchased the Billiwhack Ranch and established a dairy there in 1924. He purchased Rancho Camulos when the Del Valle family was forced to sell due to a number of mounting debts, including a host of gambling debts. (Courtesy of the Rancho Camulos Museum.)

The Fillmore depot is seen here. Many traveled from the Piru train stop to Fillmore by rail. Fruit was sent by rail to the Los Angeles markets and other points in the United States. By 1871, Rancho Camulos was producing 15,000 gallons of wine and brandy per year and would later publicize Helen Hunt Jackson's novel *Ramona* by bottling wine and labeling orange crates under the Home of Ramona label. The citrus groves consisted of 2,000 trees, including 500 walnut trees and 1,000 olive trees, and the returns were profitable. All the crops were irrigated by the Santa Clara River, with water diverted into great ditches running across the rancho. Portions of Rancho San Francisco were sold to Thomas Bard after the great drought of 1863–1864, which brought an end to the cattle era. Ulpiano Del Valle was a founder and director of the Piru Citrus Association in 1914. The Del Valles had planted the first citrus trees in the Fillmore-Piru area. The Del Valle ranch supported 200 residents with thousands of cattle, various fruits and walnuts, and acres of orange groves and vineyards. (Courtesy of the John Nichols Gallery.)

Fillmore High School students are pictured during lunchtime. Many young people attended the Piru School up to the sixth grade, and then were bused to Fillmore schools for grades seven through twelve. Everyone developed close friendships with their neighbors from Piru. (Courtesy of the Bob and Diana Cox family.)

The two Warring boys, Chester and Bennie, are seen here in the back row at right at the Piru School. (Courtesy of the Warring family.)

Juan Jose Fustero lived all his life in the Piru-Camulos area and called himself the last of the Piru Indians. He was considered the last of the full-blooded Tataviam Indians. He died on June 30, 1921, near Rancho Camulos.

The Piru Hotel, where Mary Pickford and the *Ramona* film crew spent their nights, is now known as the Round Rock Hotel, a famous landmark in Piru. (Courtesy of the Rancho Camulos Museum.)

Julius Balden settled in the Fillmore-Bardsdale area and owned the land where the Ford dealership was built. He cultivated Valencia oranges and was a well-known horticulturist.

Barbara (Balden) Jaynes was one of Julius Balden's granddaughters. Barbara and her husband, Ted Jaynes, had three girls: Kathleen, Kristine, and Karla Jaynes.

Eva Leon is pictured at the Sespe School in 1941–1942. She was sent there instead of the Mountain View School because she could speak English. There were not many Mexican Americans at the Sespe School during this time. After graduation, Eva married Larry Diaz from Santa Barbara, and they raised their children in Ventura to be close to Larry's business.

Lupe Leon Ramos is Eva Leon Diaz's younger sister. Both graduated from Fillmore schools. Eva and Lupe have had successful careers and raised families who were also successful.

Tony and Celia Diaz owned the famous Quince Letras Mexican restaurant for many years. They raised their family in Santa Paula.

Helen Soto grew up in Limoneira and attended Olivelands School. She married Manuel Gonzales and had three children, Robert, Richard, and Vela. Robert served as the Santa Paula chief of police for 33 years and was elected to the Santa Paula City Council twice, serving as mayor in 2008 and 2012.

Chet and Honor Warring lived in the Piru Mansion and were an important part of the Piru community.

Martha Gentry and John Cook are pictured at an alumni dinner in Fillmore. Martha works tirelessly as the executive director of the Fillmore Museum, and John taught mathematics for years at Fillmore High School.

Rancho Camulos workers were loyal and hardworking, from tending the cattle to picking the fruit and walnuts. Ygnacio Del Valle died in 1880 at age 72, and his wife, Ysabel, assumed control of Rancho Camulos with the help of her three sons, Reynaldo, Juventino, and Ulpiano, who raised thoroughbred horses. The Del Valles had 12 children, of whom only five lived to adulthood. Ysabel would bring orphans to live at Rancho Camulos, and it was common for up to six additional children to be staying there at any time. Dona Ysabel was living with her daughter Josefa in Los Angeles in 1905 when she passed away at the age of 68. She mourned her husband for 25 years, and before she died, she had Ygnacio's coffin dug up from the Piru Camulos Cemetery and brought to her in Los Angeles. She was buried with him in his coffin. When the funeral procession passed the Boyle Heights Orphanage, over 300 children stood outside to pay their respects to Ysabel Del Valle. (Courtesy of the Rancho Camulos Museum.)

Bibliography

Belknap, Michael. "The Era of the Lemon: A History of Santa Paula, California." *California Historical Society Quarterly* 47 (1968): 113–140.

Blanchard, Dean Hobbs. *Of California's First Citrus Empire: A Rainbow Arches from Maine to Ventura County*. Pasadena, CA: The Castle Press, 1983.

Blanchard, Sarah Eliot. *Memories of a Child's Early California Days*. Los Angeles, CA: The Ward Ritchie Press, 1961.

Camarillo, Albert. *Chicanos in a Changing Society: From Mexican Pueblos to American Barrios in Santa Barbara and Southern California, 1848–1930*. Dallas, TX: Southern Methodist University Press, 2005.

City of Santa Paula. "Original Assessment Book, City of Santa Paula, Calif." Archived in Santa Paula City Hall, 1908.

Forbes, Jack D. *Aztecas Del Norte: the Chicanos of Aztlán*. Greenwich, CT: Fawcett Publications, 1973.

McWilliams, Carey, and Matt S. Meier. *North from Mexico: the Spanish-Speaking People of the United States*. New York, NY: Greenwood Press, 1990.

Menchaca, Martha. *The Mexican Outsiders: a Community History of Marginalization and Discrimination in California*. Austin, TX: University of Texas Press, 2010.

Santa Paula Chronicle. 1910–1914, 1915–1932, 1934–1955.

Santa Paula Daily Chronicle. 1914, 1933, 1956–1986.

Santa Paula Water Works et al. v. Julio Peralta. Reel No. 38, Case No. 001458, Superior Court, Ventura County, CA: 1893–1898.

Sheridan, Edwin, ed. *History Of Ventura County*. Ventura, CA: S.J. Clark Publications, 1926.

Stansell, Ann. *Memorialization and Memory of Southern California's Forgotten St. Francis Dam Disaster of 1928*. Northridge, CA: California State University, 2014.

Stone, Mitch. *The Oaks of Santa Paula: A History of Santa Paula Canyon and the Oaks Neighborhood*. Santa Paula, CA: Fern Oaks Press, 2011.

Triem, Judith P. *Ventura County: Land of Good Fortune: an Illustrated History*. San Luis Obispo, CA: EZ Nature Books, 1990.

Ybarra, Evie. *Legendary Locals of Fillmore*. Charleston, SC: Arcadia Publishing, 2015.

INDEX

Alvarez, Irene, 74
Balden, Julius, 87, 121
Bard, Thomas, 16, 17, 18, 94, 118
Bardsdale Methodist Church, 94
Bardsdale School, 94
Bermudez, Anna Ríos, 85
Billiwhack Ranch and Dairy, 27, 28, 117
Blanchard, Ann Hobbs, 11, 12
Blanchard, Eliot, 32, 33, 34
Blanchard, Elizabeth, 33, 34, 98
Blanchard, James "Jim," 33, 34
Blanchard, John, 33, 34
Blanchard, Josephine, 32, 33
Blanchard, Nathan Weston, 9, 11, 12, 14, 17, 32, 33, 62
Blanchard, Sarah, 12, 31, 32
Briggs Packing House, 29
Briggs School, 30
Chambers Market, 55
Chess, Betsy Blanchard, 32, 33, 34
Cook, John, 124
Cox, Diana Nichols, 100, 104
Cummings, Richard, 59
Diaz, Celia and Tony, 123
Diaz, Eva (Leon), 122
Dickenson, Don, 76
Del Valle family, 9, 111, 113, 114, 115, 117, 118
Del Valle, Reynaldo, 9, 113, 114, 125
Edmunds, Lynda, 89
Fansler, Vesta, 48
Fillmore Fish Hatchery, 92
Fogata, Robert, 60
Fox Theater, 53
Galvin, Mary, 30, 110
Gentry, Martha, 124
Glen Tavern Inn, 11, 36, 52
Godoy, Linda Gonzalez, 84
Goodenough family, 88
Gonzales, Helen (Soto), 73, 123
Gonzalez, Irene, 84, 105
Gonzalez, Richard, 105
Gonzalez, Robert, 123
Gottardi family, 38
Hardison, Wallace L., 9, 15, 16, 19, 20, 46, 51, 63
Hearst, Phoebe, 115
Hume, Chief Earl, 100
Isbell School, 37, 55, 72
Jauregui Ranch, 29
Jaynes, Barbara (Balden), 121
Jones, Laurabelle, 88
Jones, Stan, 88
Jue family, 54, 59, 74
Jue's Superette, 54
Keene, Herman, 21, 48
Kelly, Peggy, 52
Limoneira 9, 11, 22–26, 29, 30, 64, 92, 123
Lopez family, 49, 107
Lummis, Charles, 114, 115
McKevett, Charles H., 16, 49
McKinley, Patrick, 107
Marquez family, 47, 71
Michel family, 57, 95
Monahan, Kevin, 108
Morales, Ernie and Becky, 93
More, T. Wallace, 9, 11, 77, 78
More, Susannah de Ortega, 78, 79
Olivelands School, 30, 73, 110, 123
Patterson family, 103, 104
Ramirez, Dr. Richard "Ricky," 85
Ramos, Lupe (Leon), 122
Romero family, 58, 81, 86
Rubel family, 27, 117
St. Francis Dam disaster, 35–42, 72, 88, 96
Sanchez, Abundio 81, 116
Sanchez, Concepción, 81–85, 116
Sanitary Dairy, 9, 90
Santa Paula Airport, 56, 57
Santa Paula Chronicle, 52, 53
Santa Paula High School, 33, 73, 74, 75, 76
Shiells family, 89, 90, 100
Shively, Doug, 61
Sing family, 62
Spalding, Albert, 79, 93
Spalding, Eudora, 9, 79, 93
Spalding, Keith, 9, 79, 93
Starnes, Jack, 90
Surdam, Royce G., 17, 97
Teague family, 46, 47, 95
Victoria family, 60, 67
Villa, Joe, 61
Villasenor, Dave and Sharon, 89
Ybarra, Brandon, 106
Ybarra, Eddie, 89
Ybarra, Minnie, 34, 98
Ybarra, Marcelino "Woody," 34, 98, 105, 106, 110
Ybarra, Soledad (Sanchez), 81, 85
Watkins Hardware, 54
Warring family, 100, 111, 119, 124
Wilson, Roy Sr., 55, 72
Winkler, Monty and Maio, 47, 95

Discover Thousands of Local History Books Featuring Millions of Vintage Images

Arcadia Publishing, the leading local history publisher in the United States, is committed to making history accessible and meaningful through publishing books that celebrate and preserve the heritage of America's people and places.

Find more books like this at
www.arcadiapublishing.com

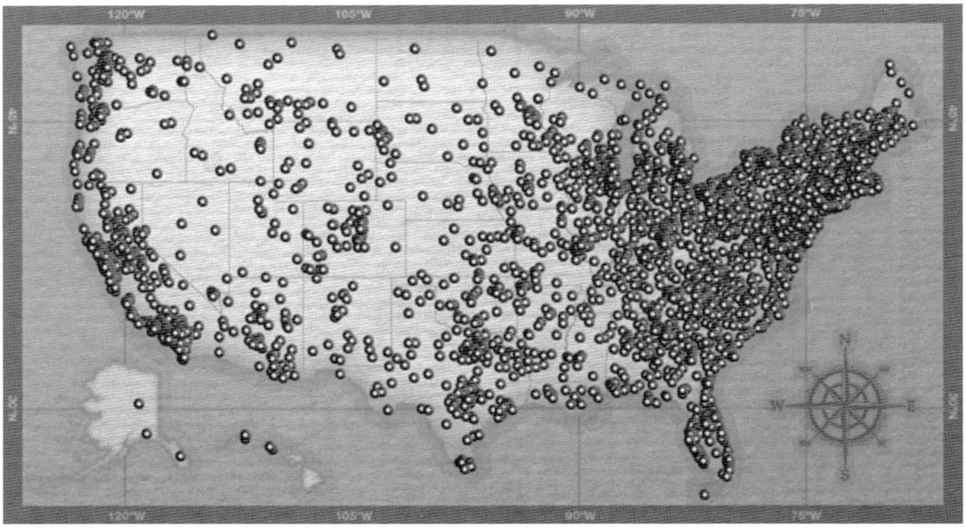

Search for your hometown history, your old stomping grounds, and even your favorite sports team.

Consistent with our mission to preserve history on a local level, this book was printed in South Carolina on American-made paper and manufactured entirely in the United States. Products carrying the accredited Forest Stewardship Council (FSC) label are printed on 100 percent FSC-certified paper.

MADE IN THE USA